Biblical Responsible Investing

"Don't pick up this book – instead, buy a handful and start studying it together with a few others who are serious about following Jesus in their finances as in every other part of their lives! This little book is dynamite, totally readable, and will help every reader to understand why it is, as Jesus said, 'more blessed to give than to receive.'"

— **Dr. Tony Dale,** Founder and Board Chairman of Sedera

"Wow! If you have a passion to be a good steward of the resources you've been blessed with, then read this book. The title is *Biblical Responsible Investing*, and it leaves you not only motivated but inspired. Thank you, Darryl, for sharing your wisdom unashamedly."

— **Michael D. Perkins,** CPA, CFP®, Managing Partner & CEO of Slattery Perkins Ramirez

"With perceptivity to evangelical Christianity and the world of finance, Darryl Lyons has written a compelling book that addresses current trends in both. Anyone interested in the financial decisions of money-conscious evangelicals would do well to read this book. Genuine and knowledgeable, Darryl writes with an accessible, clear, and entertaining style."

— **Andrew Riley,** Ph.D., College App 101

"Darryl Lyons uses compelling stories and practical examples to show readers how their faith can guide them toward smart and intentional financial decisions. If you don't like reading about money, this book will change your mind."

— **Rachel Schnoll,** CEO, Jewish Communal Fund

"Do you assume one size fits all when servicing the Christian marketplace? Darryl Lyons helps you understand why that's a mistake, clarifies the nuances in a practical, easy to access manner, and gives you practical tips for your success with this consumer group."

— **Dr. Joey Faucette,** GodNods.Today

"Darryl sees the big picture and brings a wit and wisdom down to us Earthlings who are just passing through. So, since we're here, let's use every tool we can to be in the world but not of it. *Biblical Responsible Investing* was probably written on the Isle of Patmos – it's prophetic and practical. Darryl backs up his observations with The Word, and that's the bottom line. Most authors would give you 10 Trends That Will Impact Faithful Americans . . . Darryl takes it to 11."

— **Baron Wiley,** President, Bofars Media Group

"Finance is an arena of faith expression and exercise, and the trends Darryl guides you through are relevant for anyone looking to be intentional with money matters!"

— **Mike Sharrow,** CEO, The C12 Group

"As a second-generation family business owner, I appreciate how Darryl's words have helped me reflect on the conflicts many Christian businessowners face. We want to grow, we want to be successful, but *for what purpose*, and *to what end*? Is money just there to fuel even more consumption *or* can wise stewardship help us create more opportunity? Grateful for a courageous voice in this critical financial space."

— **Tonya Christal,** DDS, Co-owner of Lee Dental Centers

"What's beautiful about this book is that it accomplishes two very important tasks. The first was definitely one of Darryl's goals, to point out how differently a Christian views money. However, it also accomplishes another important task . . . to make us Christians re-examine ourselves in light of how we know we should be viewing money, but sometimes fall short in our daily living. The book is bold and convicting, but tempered with kindness and understanding along the way."

— **Mark Goldman,** CPA, Business Strategist

"In *Biblical Responsible Investing*, Darryl illuminates several opportunities Christian men and women can employ to be better stewards of the resources ultimately received from God. If you are searching for answers on how to responsibly grow a legacy for your family in a God-honoring fashion, give Darryl's latest book a read. The principles discussed in its pages will help you factor your faith into your finances and arm you with effective strategies to consider incorporating into your financial planning."

— **Nathan Ketterling,** Attorney

"No matter your religious or political affiliation, *Biblical Responsible Investing* is a refreshingly enjoyable and thought-provoking read, filled with pearls of wisdom on how to live a more fulfilling life based on Christian principles and motivation to serve a higher purpose."

— **Brian Thorp,** Wealthtender CEO

"In reading this book, I realized that I am not alone! In an effort to quiet my voice, the world wants me to feel isolated and wonder if anyone else actually believes as I do when it comes to my financial worldview. This book shows the power for good that we as Christians have as a cohesive unit in making financial decisions based on the teachings of our LORD."

— **Sherri Smith,** Ministry Volunteer

"Darryl provides a thorough overview of financial issues as well as solutions and resources in a very user-friendly language with a Christian worldview. Having almost fifty years' experience in financial matters from a Christian worldview myself, I would recommend this resource to everyone young, old, and in between, from novice to professional. You will be enlightened and blessed."

— **Bruce Barnard,** Chairman, BDI Insurance

"Darryl creatively redirects our heart to focus on something bigger than personal wealth accumulation. When I lose focus on the good and become distracted from my purpose, I reflect on Matthew 6:21: 'For where your treasure is, there your heart will be also.'"

— **George Mentz,** Graduate Law Professor, Texas A&M University School of Law

Insights for Kingdom-Minded Investors

BIBLICAL RESPONSIBLE INVESTING

DARRYL W. LYONS

NASHVILLE

NEW YORK • LONDON • MELBOURNE • VANCOUVER

Biblical Responsible Investing

Insights for Kingdom-Minded Investors

Published in New York, New York, by Morgan James Publishing. Morgan James is a trademark of Morgan James, LLC. www.MorganJamesPublishing.com

Proudly distributed by Publishers Group West®

All Scripture quotations are taken from the Holy Bible, New International Version, NIV. Copyright ©, 1973, 1978, 1984, 2011 by Biblica, Inc.

Morgan James BOGO™

A FREE ebook edition is available for you or a friend with the purchase of this print book.

CLEARLY SIGN YOUR NAME ABOVE

Instructions to claim your free ebook edition:
1. Visit MorganJamesBOGO.com
2. Sign your name CLEARLY in the space above
3. Complete the form and submit a photo of this entire page
4. You or your friend can download the ebook to your preferred device

ISBN 9781636982212 paperback
ISBN 9781636982229 ebook
Library of Congress Control Number:
2023937824

Cover & Interior Design by:
Christopher Kirk
www.GFSstudio.com

Morgan James PUBLISHING

Builds

with...

Habitat for Humanity®
Peninsula and Greater Williamsburg

Morgan James is a proud partner of Habitat for Humanity Peninsula and Greater Williamsburg. Partners in building since 2006.

Get involved today! Visit: www.morgan-james-publishing.com/giving-back

To: Caresse, Luke, Claire, Noelle, and Lucy. My Lyons Den.

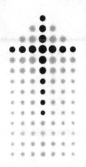

Acknowledgments

Thank you to the entire PAX Financial Group team for radiating teamwork, respect, enthusiasm, constant improvement, and kindness. Special appreciation to Janise Brooks for her going above and beyond in literally everything. Michelle Booth for the editing and finishing my thoughts. Tina Beck for marketing/publishing support and encouragement for this initiative. Morgan James for the continued publishing partnership and aligned mission. So many friends and family to name who give me confidence when I doubt myself. I sincerely appreciate you.

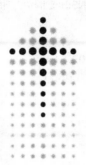

Table of Contents

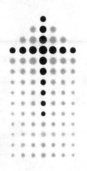

Preface

I remember it like it was yesterday. My high-school friends and I had piled into a rusty old Ford Bronco and were racing down the Texas backroads just north of Mexico. We drove parallel to the waterways (also known as resacas) irrigating Rio Grande Valley farmlands. The lyrics from Alice in Chains' hit song "Rooster" blared in the background. Back then, most of us boys left school on Friday after football practice to go to the beaches on South Padre Island. The Bronco's seats were torn, and the dashboard had cracks, but cosmetics weren't a priority for seventeen-year-olds. We just needed something to take us away from high school football fields and to the beaches before sunset.

As we sped by the small Texas towns, my blond-haired buddy, Alan, yelled over the guitar riffs, "Do you know what this song's about?" I had no clue, even though I always sang every word. Alan filled me in. "It's about Vietnam, man. It's about surviving the war. You know, people died, and many men were lost in the jungles, wounded, never to see their families again." I responded gently, "Wow . . . that's deep." I didn't have a clue. Maybe I should have paid closer attention to the words or read the inside of the CD cover.

When we returned home from the beach, now motivated by curiosity, I digested Alice in Chains. The lead singer, Layne Staley, could do no wrong in my book. Despite the heroin addiction he suffered, his profound, dark poetry laced with an alternative metal sound was a gift to the world. On a bad day, I would absorb the vocals of "Rooster," "Them Bones," or "Dam That River." Screaming Layne's lyrics made life feel a little better.

One song that struck a chord with me was called "Man in the Box." In this song, Layne talked about Jesus. Now, I've always loved Jesus since I was a little boy. That's how my momma raised me. My friends and I left for the beaches on

Friday, but we all went to church on Wednesday. Admittedly, we went there for the girls, but despite our ulterior motivations at the time, we still absorbed some of the sermons. With my newfound Alice in Chains insight, now those sermons clashed with my boy Layne Staley and his "Man in the Box" lyrics.

Just after Layne growls the name Jesus Christ, the backup vocals echo in the background, "Deny your maker." That's odd; is he talking about Jesus?

Let me play it again.

Sure enough, "Deny your maker." Does this mean I need to burn the album, or I'll go to hell? What would the pastor say? How do I reconcile my next favorite Alice in Chains song, "God Smack"? Or, as I dug further, all the other "non-Christian" Layne Staley lyrics? I can't love Jesus and then, at the same time, sing, "Deny my maker." Can I? But I can't abandon my boy either; I love Layne and his music . . . it's my go-to when I'm struggling with my self-worth. At seventeen, I relate to Layne's flannel more than the preacher's hair part. I have conflicting thoughts. I have conflicting desires. At seventeen, I have a foot in two different worlds. One world, the Layne Staley world, seems annoyed and irritated by the idea of Jesus, whereas my local church claims that only true life comes from knowing your Maker. I'm struggling to reconcile these worldviews.

Fast-forward to two decades later. I'm in my mid-forties, and I've chosen one of the worldviews: Christianity. I am comfortable with what faith tells me about where I came from, my purpose, and where I am going. Don't get me wrong, this view of the world is messy in how it manifests in my life, but if you were to peel back my motivation for how I live and raise my family, it is often rooted in the Christian worldview.

We often think about our view of the world solely within an array of stained-glass church windows, but I'm encouraged by the movement of those integrating their authentic worldview outside the church walls. As I've matured in my faith, this worldview has even determined how I do my work. I've counseled thousands about personal finances for over two decades, from a stage to a simulcast to television. Every day, someone emails or calls me with a question about money. Now, my answer is rooted in my Christian worldview, which helps me ask better questions, such as, "Do you give because you want to reduce your taxes or because it is important to your faith?" Maybe it's both. Or "Do you save because you are worried about the future or something you read in the Bible?"

There is a massive movement of Christians adopting a Christian worldview with the most potent force on the planet: money. There is much legacy to work from. The Bible expresses this worldview, where two thousand money scriptures for over two thousand years have provided time-tested wisdom on aligning money with a unique life purpose. With all the contradicting American messages about money, I find it refreshing to make even money decisions with a Christian worldview top of mind.

Can I say I'm perfect at separating my Christian worldview from the allure of American consumerism? Nope, I still enjoy nice shoes and going out to eat; heck, I'll even catch myself binge-shopping on Amazon. But my sincere motivation is aligned with thousands of other passionate people committed to purposely filtering daily decisions, including money, through a Christian worldview.

Continuing the Conversation

The original manuscript for this book was intended for my friends on Wall Street and those grinding it out in the corporate world. I sensed that my Wall Street friends were completely underestimating the economic influence of the Christian community. After multiple kneecap to kneecap conversations, my assumptions were proven right. Through this book and more respectful dialogue, we can provide Wall Street with insight into the Christian community's very unique relationship with money. I hope corporate America resets its assumptions and arrives at a place where they sincerely appreciate, respect, and honor the Christian community's money motivations.

As a fundamental side note, when I developed the manuscript for this book, I realized that the non-business Christian community would benefit from peeking behind the Wall Street investment curtain. So, after about five edits, Biblical Responsible Investing evolved. I reduced some Wall Street jargon, adjusted terminology, and made it more readable for the non-business-person. Additional thoughts will be found in the "Continuing the Conversation" sections at the end of each chapter. This revised content will help the non-business reader understand what is happening in the financial world. With this insight, you can play a role in ensuring the Christian voice is heard.

"He changes times and seasons; he deposes kings
and raises up others. He gives wisdom to the wise
and knowledge to the discerning."

Daniel 2:21

Biblically Responsible Investing (BRI), is a Christian movement that aims to align our investments with Biblical values. To learn more about BRI visit: https://paxfinancialgroup.com/biblically-responsible-investing/

Biblically Responsible Investing ("BRI") involves, among other things, screening for companies that fit within the goal of investing in companies aligned with biblical values. Such screens may serve to reduce the pool of high-performing companies considered for investment. Investing involves risk. BRI investing does not guarantee a favorable investment outcome.

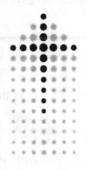

CHAPTER 1:

Political Motivations

C hristians have decided that the two major political parties don't match their values and are turning in their political badges. Christian voters who identify as Republican have declined from 87% in 2008 to 80% in 2019.

Now, let's not get too excited, my blue-state friends.

During that same period, Christians who identify as Democrats have dropped from 73% to 51%.[i] If Christians leave both parties, it's less important to ask, "Where are they going?" and, more importantly, ask, "Why are they disassociating from political parties? What is their motivation to abandon their previous political loyalties?"

The word "motivation" comes from the Latin *movere*, which means "to move". Motivation asks, "What 'moves' someone to start something, stop something, or continue?" What thought lights up in a person's head before they take action? Unfortunately (or fortunately), thoughts aren't transparent to others, and no one is a mind reader. So, futile human beings trip up and misjudge people's motivations, often defaulting to presume the worst intention.

Christians have dealt with this misinterpretation of their motivations for centuries, and today's politics amplify the misunderstanding. For that reason, I need to get something out of the way, Christians are not Democrats, Republicans, or MAGAs.

We'll unpack the trend within the Christian money movement. But let's not get lost in humanity along the journey. Despite all the tribes in the world, such as LGBTQ+, Evangelicals, the Climate Change community, MAGA, BLM, or a mix and match of the above, we all share in our humankind. Despite the different motivations that I'll point out in this text, most of us still say, "Ouch," (or some other four-letter word) when we touch a hot stove, lose sleep over our kids' future, and want to get a fair shake in this world. Unfortunately, where we find ourselves today, our humanity has been hijacked by a shadow of passionate politics that blackens our core commonalities. And it seems social media's job description is to keep us perpetually offended.

Republican and Democrat politicians are masters at upsetting people, and it's often the modus operandi so that they can stand out, build a tribe, and be the solution. They usually grab religious people by the ear, pull them into their tribe, and get them fired up about the latest issue. But religious people aren't thinking, "Hey, today I want to upset or offend someone because that's what my religion teaches me."

Religion teaches people to be much more reflective and introspective, but as with any belief system, it can and will offend others because it is built upon a framework of rights and wrongs. But thank God for America because regardless of anyone's theistic point of view, religion is still very sacred and a protected right in our country. The Equal Employment Opportunity Commission (EEOC) aims to preserve religion and defines it as a belief system with "ultimate questions having to do with deep and imponderable matters." [ii]

For many, religion is a systematic explanation that orders one's life. Throughout the text, we often reference this idea of explaining life as a "worldview."

Now that we have separated a Christian worldview from political stereotypes let's explore a little more about what these Christians are all about. Christians in the first century were known as people of the Way. These people of the Way believed that Jesus Christ died, was resurrected from death on the cross, and was, in fact, the son of God. Before his death, Jesus Christ taught much about the "ultimate questions having to do with deep and imponderable matters." Many of these teachings (often through parables) were the complete opposite of the popular and mainstream culture in the early first century. For example, if you get punched, he said to turn the other cheek; he taught that giving is better than receiving, and he even discussed the futility of chasing worldly riches. It is no wonder these early Christians were called people of the Way. Their way was vastly different from the first-century Roman and the traditional Jewish way of life that made wealth, pleasures, and rules a priority.

Two thousand years later, Christianity has survived genocide and severe global persecution and still lives out this counter-cultural way of life, including a different way of thinking about money. Now there is an entire movement of Christians focused on aligning their values with their wallet, and it has my attention because the magnitude is significant.

Why do politicians patronize Christians? Because Christians are one of the wealthiest groups of people in the world. In fact, according to The Economic Times, Christians hold 55% of the world's wealth [iii] and are becoming much more intentional about where the money is going. But we run into a significant problem when evaluating the money behaviors of the Christian community. The greatest challenge is that it is socially acceptable and, in some pockets, "cool" to identify as a Christian in America.

Most people check the Christian box because they go to church on Easter and think Jesus is a good guy, yet they have no other tangible alignment with the Christian community's deeply held values and convictions. According to Barna Research, 70% of Americans identify as Christians, but we scratch our heads wondering why 70% of Christians don't act like it. [iv] The imperfect but best way to know who in America is "all-in" on their Christian faith is by their actions. As they say, actions speak louder than words. So, we'll look at a group beyond social Christians or even the political Christians and explore a subset, a narrower group called "Practicing Christians."

We'll use The American Bible Society's explanation of a Practicing Christian, defined as someone who "identifies as a Christian, attends a religious service at least once a month," and whose "faith is essential" in their life. [v]

Some data is available on how large this population could be among the American people, but it isn't easy to quantify and is very fluid. However, for this conversation, we will focus on this nebulous group of Christians whose firmly held beliefs are reflected in their actions were once called the people of the Way and are now considered Practicing Christians. We will use the terms Practicing Christian and Christian interchangeably throughout this text, referring to those who believe "faith to be essential" to their daily lives, not those who consider Christianity a passive (or political) part of their lives.

We may never know the overlap or the subset numbers exactly. Still, I can attest Practicing Christians are not made up of the political characters that Don Lemon or Sean Hannity highlight. This group of Practicing Christians holds fast to the principles of the faith and gathers to be very intentional with its resources. You will begin to see the unique motivations and behaviors of this defined group called Practicing Christians. Now that we have distinguished between Practicing Christians and the political talking heads' definition of Christians, we'll examine how this movement of Practicing Christians is extremely motivated to play a completely different money game than the rest of America.

Especially when it comes to the "American dream."

Continuing the Conversation

I'll define and redefine Christians throughout this book, but it will be tough to digest the content in Biblical Responsible Investing if we can't disconnect politics from faith. I've had many liberal, conservative, atheist, and Christian friends preview this book in its early sloppy manuscript days. I discovered that learning about Christian money motivations will be challenging if the reader can't disconnect from what they absorbed from CNN and Fox News. As you continue reading, do your best to view Christians from a non-political point of view, and the content will be easier to absorb and make much more sense.

> "No one can serve two masters. Either you will hate one and love the other, or you will be devoted to the one and despise the other. You cannot serve both God and money."
> *Matthew 6:24*

CHAPTER 2:

Checkers vs. Chess

B ecause Christians tend to live among the culture, buy the same clothes at Target, eat chips and salsa, and often enjoy the same beer as everyone else, we assume they think the same way. Practicing Christians are hard to spot because they walk among us without long dresses, burqas, or other outward distinguishing characteristics. Even their transactional money behaviors are similar, such as saving in a 401(k), using a debit card, or buying life insurance. But don't confuse those transactional similarities with the significant motivational differences. It is often the motivation of money that matters, and if Christians are playing the game of money like chess, the rest of the world is playing money like checkers. This is not to point out that one game is more intelligent than another; instead, it is the reality that Christians play a completely different game with their money, and no one acknowledges the difference. The financial community continues to tell all of us (including Christians) to become multimillionaires, retire at our second vacation home, and laugh at the world because we won the game of life. That's the American dream, but not the Christian one.

The American money dream directly conflicts with Christians' deeply held convictions. For example, Christians believe their money is not theirs; they believe everything they have and own is a gift from God. The secular world seems more logical because there the money likely belongs to the name that appears on the bank account. This is not to say that Christians don't recognize the legal framework of our financial systems; they just don't hold their money with a tight fist. They are thankful for what they have because money can be fleeting, and when it goes, they are at peace (or at least should be).

Another example of the contrasting money perspective is regarding personal pleasures. Like many, Christians enjoy fine dining, a comfortable bed, or even fast cars. The difference is that Christians don't make personal pleasure the primary goal of obtaining wealth. Christians believe that the way they treat their money reflects their hearts. As a result, they make generosity a priority above personal pleasure.

So, what is the motivation for money for Christians? It is to honor their God, reflected in loving a neighbor; this is the golden rule. What is the general American consumer's motivation? Whoever has the gold rules.

Therein lie two contrasting money motivators.

We must distinguish between these two belief systems and recognize that the ultimate motive of the Christian community is stewardship, which is the care of something that doesn't belong to someone. For example, imagine when a secular realtor is trying to sell a million-dollar vacation home to a Christian and makes the wrong assumption about the motivation of that Christian. The realtor can quickly get frustrated when the Christian doesn't take this great deal. The realtor may offer concessions on closing costs, furniture, or a substantial discount on the asking price. How could the Christian not jump on this? The Christian shouldn't lose out on a good deal, indeed. Being stupid for Jesus is still stupid. But the non-Christian agent must recognize that a vacation home at a reasonable price may conflict with the Christian motivation for stewardship. In the Christian's prayer time, they will be asking, "Lord, is this what you want me to do with your resources?" or "Have you given me a vision for this vacation home to honor and serve you?" If those questions remained unanswered, the Christian buyer might walk away from the deal leaving the seller bewildered and possibly angry. Like all of us, the seller will manufacture some negative story in his head about the motivation of the Christian buyer. The realtor is playing checkers, and the Christian is playing chess, which is often why these missed motivations can make relationships sour. Knowing that stewardship is the essence of a Christian's motivation will bridge the gap of misunderstanding in nearly all transactions.

We will discover how corporate America can intersect, collide, and sometimes conflict with this Christian worldview as we dig further.

Continuing the Conversation

I should probably write more on American consumerism, but that topic is a book by itself. But it's worth noting that we are addicted to the dopamine hit enjoyed by clicking the "buy now" button and the subsequent arrival of every Amazon box. It doesn't matter if you are a Christian or a non-Christian; this dopamine hit is a shared addiction, robbing us of giving and saving. Consumerism continues to be a growing trend for all Americans. To avoid consumer addiction, practice pausing before the purchase.

> *"Better a little with righteousness*
> *than much gain with injustice."*
> *Proverbs 16:8*

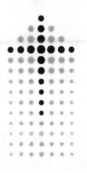

CHAPTER 3:

Disowning Corporations

The ancient texts guide Christians and encourage them to save for the future. Saving for the future was necessary for sustaining life and was reinforced by the authors of these texts. Many who wrote and read the passages were farmers in an agricultural economy with unpredictable weather. Today, we may have more visibility through a doppler radar, but when it comes to our health and financial future, all of our crystal balls are cracked and cloudy. Despite our technological innovations, we don't know if we'll die soon from a meteor crashing through the roof or live to 105 holding hands with our spouse in bed. Because of this uncertainty coupled with longer life expectancies, the Christian community (besides a few subcultures) generally aligns with American culture's desperate need to invest for retirement, college, or rainy days.

However, what is changing is not the amount to invest but where to invest those dollars. For many of us, the stock market has been the tool of choice to build wealth. I would suggest that capital markets have been one of the most incredible wealth-generating inventions in human history. Think about it. Six hundred or seven hundred years ago, if you were a peasant and, even worse, a serf, there wasn't a single mechanism to build wealth for you, your children, and your children's children. The stock market changed that and gave people a tool to build generational wealth.

The problem for Christians is not the stock market or financial innovations. What has become a considerate pebble in the shoe for many Christians is investing in companies that are antithetical to their sincerely held religious convictions. The movement of refusing to knowingly invest in companies that use profits to undermine a Christian worldview is proliferating.

Christians refuse to profit from companies that use their earnings to support legislation restricting religious freedom.

Now, this pain point isn't altogether new. In the eighteenth century, some religious investing groups took issue with alcohol, tobacco, and gambling and excluded those companies from their investment portfolio. But because of today's political and polarized environment, the bifurcation of American values stands out now more than ever. Online content offered by Disney, Netflix, and others has recently troubled Christians, and Christian consumers have voted with their wallets. The hashtag #BoycottDisney gained significant momentum, causing the company to reduce its long-term subscriber forecast by fifteen million in its guidance to shareholders.[vi]

Christians have voted with their spending dollars but are also beginning to vote with their investment dollars. The appetite for company accountability is accelerating, and asset managers have responded by leveraging financial technology to develop robust algorithms that screen out companies behaving in a way that undermines Christian values. This method is known as Biblically Responsible Investing (BRI).

Biblically Responsible Investing is the process of investing in a basket of stocks, mutual funds, or other securities that are aligned with a Christian worldview. Some companies would be screened out of a BRI portfolio because their business is tied to pornography or alcohol. Alternatively, some companies that may be favorably adopted into a BRI portfolio have a track record of fair wages and selling products that help rather than hurt people. Christians want to root for a company to win and are no longer becoming indifferent to the cognitive dissonance when dividend checks come at the expense of religious values.

Many investment firms are entering the space to help Christians, and many of these screens vary from asset manager to asset manager. When I was first introduced to BRI, I listed out (in Excel) every value of conviction to my faith and worldview. Then, I interviewed values-based managers to see who had adopted my screens without deviation.

I was disappointed to learn that no asset manager wholly aligned with my convictions (go figure . . . no one agrees with me 100 percent of the time).

After getting over my dogmatic approach to BRI screens, I realized that there are various denominations, methods, and techniques to screens, and the best system is the one that "mostly" fits someone's values. The good news is that many asset managers' choices have emerged in recent years. Some develop their entire product offering around BRI. At the same time, other purely secular firms have caught on to the Christian investing movement and have carved out an investment portfolio for those who desire a faith-based investing approach. Those secular investment firms aren't dummies; they know where the money is and are willing to honor and respect Christian motivations. It might be a smart business model despite some secular pushback from a small group of people who disagree with the Christian value system.

Another concern in my initial research was the sacrifice of performance. However, much data has identified that there is little or no trade-off in performance. For example, RBC Global Asset Management consolidated many studies within the broad universe of socially responsible types of investments. It said that "the chief finding of this research is that socially responsible investing does not result in lower investment returns." [vii]Also, to be more specific, The Christian Investment Forum's 2020 Study found a slight outperformance with the Biblically Responsible Investing universe within the large-cap stock space. [viii]We'll continue to monitor ongoing studies, but the data so far is encouraging that those motivated by investing with a BRI screen are not sacrificing performance.

Of course, if we take this Biblically Responsible Investing conviction to the extreme, all Christians would live in isolation surrounded by Bubble Wrap (only made by Christians, of course). However, that isn't practical nor aligned with biblical theology that states Christians should be "in the world" but not "of the world." At the very least, it is prudent to honor and respect the growing movement of Christian shareholders who want to avoid investing retirement dollars in companies that use profits to undermine Christian values altogether.

Next, we'll look at how the power of intentional charitable giving.

Continuing the Conversation

Check with your advisor, bank, or financial institution. Many big Wall Street firms are afraid to offer Biblically Responsible Investing (BRI). They love their Environmental, Social, and Governance (ESG) strategies but fear offending the loud voices if they offer faith-based investing. If your bank or investment firm doesn't offer BRI, you may want to rethink your financial partner because that institution likely has very different values than you.

"In everything I did, I showed you that by this kind
of hard work we must help the weak, remembering
the words the Lord Jesus himself said: 'It is more
blessed to give than to receive.'"
Acts 20:35

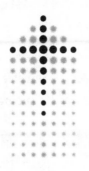

CHAPTER 4:

Charitable Giving

Practicing Christians give more money to charity.

In the State of the Bible Report for 2022 from the American Bible Society, Americans who regularly engage in the Bible gave $145 billion to charities (not just churches) in 2021, which accounted for about $2,907 in giving per household. Thought of another way, Practicing Christians, who "represent 19% of US adults, are responsible for giving 44% of every dollar donated by individuals nationwide."[ix] Because of the significant difference in the amount and the potential collective global economic impact, we'll need to critically unpack the Practicing Christian's motivation behind giving.

One of the critical central tenets of the Christian faith is that finances reflect one's heart. For example, if someone hoards money, this likely indicates a deep-rooted fear that developed from growing up with an empty pantry and holes in one's shoes. Alternatively, someone addicted to luxuries may struggle with insecurity and feels that glitter and gold gives them a sense of worth. Or, if an employer doesn't pay a fair wage, you could assume greed exists. Don't be confused; it's not that money is the root of all evil. Instead, it's the love of money that's the root of all evil. It comes down to motivation. The Christian worldview is less concerned with actions but rather is more concerned with motivation. This idea makes it difficult for outsiders to pass judgment. For example, if a Christian is motivated to give to an inner-city building project, an outsider with a different worldview might conclude that the Christian motivation was to get recognition, a pat on the back, or a tax deduction. Now, for some, that may be partially or even entirely true. However, from my experience and my many years working with Christians, I would make the case that motivations to give are generally sincere and aligned with a desire to be a steward, love a neighbor, and honor their Creator.

The idea of giving is often motivated by a place of altruism, which should be a byproduct of the Christian faith. Christians are generally not inspired to give to get their name on a building or receive a round of applause (nothing wrong here). So often, Christian giving is done in the shadows without anyone knowing the true source. That is why many people materially discount the global impact of the Christian community, who usually have the money ready to make things happen. Pay attention to future natural disasters and international needs from now on. You will see that Christians are the first ones at the site of a domestic hurricane disaster long before the Red Cross or the first to invest in a water well in Africa before any government official has even thought about it.

The collective church preaches a 10% tithe; this is not unreasonable if a person lives within their means. There is debate on "How much?" and "To whom?" Other internal discussions include the following: Should the 10% be pre-tax or post-tax income? Is the tithe to the church you attend? If so, what about para churches such as street-corner preachers, pregnancy care centers, or missionaries? I will set those debates aside for now because, often, those are individual decisions. And, in the end, as I continue to repeat myself, it is a matter of the heart.

But let's not forget about the tax deduction.

Christians should be strategic in their giving to reduce their taxable income. We should pay the IRS, but no one needs to leave a tip. First, the Qualified Charitable Distribution (QCD) is a very effective tool for money to be transferred from an Individual Retirement Arrangement (IRA) to a 501(c)(3) nonprofit organization.[x] A person must distribute the required minimum (RMD) at a defined age provided by the IRS. The RMD is calculated using the IRS Published Life Expectancy Tables. [xi] This information will be reported to the IRA owner on Form 1099-R and, if under the annual limits, will not result in a taxable distribution. If the IRA owner doesn't use the QCD and pays the charity directly from their bank account, this could negatively impact cash flow.

Let's nerd into math for a second; I won't keep you here long. Suppose someone didn't know about the QCD but still wanted to give $10,000 to his favorite charity. He would withdraw $10,000 from the IRA and withhold 20% (depending on the bracket) or $2,000 in income. Then, suppose the IRA owner files his tax return, and his standard deduction is higher than his itemized deduction. In that case, he will not have a corresponding $10,000 itemized charitable tax deduction to

offset his $10,000 IRA withdrawal. As a result of not know-
ing the QCD was an option, this IRA owner inadvertently
paid $2,000 more in taxes. A QCD sends the money directly
from the IRA to the charity, bypassing the individual's taxable
income altogether.

Donor-Advised Funds (DAFs) are another unique strategy for charitably inclined people. A DAF is helpful to a
person who wants to give to a charity but is passionately torn
between two or three nonprofits and needs more time to delib-
erate. But this person also needs to receive a tax deduction in
the current year to offset income. In this situation, the charitably inclined person could contribute to a DAF and receive an
immediate calendar-year deduction. This deduction is considered an itemized deduction and does not translate into a benefit unless it exceeds the standard deduction ($12,950 for single
filers and $25,900 for joint filers in 2022).[xii] The donor can
usually deduct cash donations (checks, wire transfers, etc.) up
to 60% of his adjusted gross income.

However, one nuance that requires more diligence when set-
ting up a DAF for a Christian is finding the right company to take
custody of the assets. There has been increasing pushback against
Christian organizations whose deeply held beliefs are being
characterized as hateful or racist. One organization that attempts
to influence the Fidelity Charitable Donor-Advised Fund is a

grassroots organization called Unmasking Fidelity. In its letter to Fidelity, it falsely claims that several Christian organizations "promote rhetoric and policies that enable white-supremacist and fascist violence." [xiii] Suppose Fidelity or other secular organizations react to these voices. In that case, those with DAFS may find that their distributions could be restricted or made publicly available when the DAF is specifically designed to keep distributions private. Several DAF custodians have recognized this potential threat and are positioned to honor and respect Christians. There is movement within the Christian community to use only DAFS that will align with a Christian worldview. Christians want to know that their monies will be safely stewarded by organizations deeply rooted in their faith. DAF custodians are revising their marketing to stand out from their larger secular counterparts. I have noticed more and more investors recognizing the distinction between custodians and making their investment choice based on the custodian that aligns with the Christian worldview.

We want to recognize a Christian's desire to give while identifying ways to reduce taxable income. If possible, we should be aware of any product solution or custodian threats that have taken adverse positions against Christians. Christians are motivated by giving, not primarily for the tax deduction or even the recognition (although that may play a role), but rather by the sincere desire to be a good steward, love their neighbor, and honor their Creator.

What hurts giving? Medical bills. In the next section, we'll see how innovative Christians have found an alternative to traditional health insurance.

Continuing the Conversation

Have you noticed that our country is struggling with anxiety? According to the University of Notre Dame Science of Generosity, there is a direct correlation between giving financially and anxiety reduction.[xiv] In fact, as I read the Bible (Malachi 3:10), God says, "Test me in this." In other words, test God by being generous and watch what happens. Those "test me" words are powerful, and I don't take them lightly. If you aren't a giver yet, I would encourage you to test God over the next year and see what happens. You'll be surprised that your bills will still be paid, you'll still make memories, and, at the same time (through your giving), the hungry will have an extra meal. The only pain may be fewer Amazon boxes on your doorstep.

"Carry each other's burdens, and in this way, you will fulfill the law of Christ."

Galatians 6:2

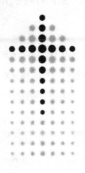

CHAPTER 5:

Scraping Traditional Health Insurance

I n counseling thousands of Christians about money over the years, I have only met a few people who don't buy health insurance because they believe God will care for everything. Those Christians are the exception. Most Christians recognize the value of protecting their family's health by outsourcing their medical risks to an organization that can afford to pay a cancer claim.

But a new insurance alternative for Christians has emerged in the last several decades. This phenomenon gained considerable attention when Obama signed the Affordable Care Act (ACA). As a result of this legislation, premiums for the middle class accelerated. There were some beneficial features of the bill (tax subsidies, everyone's insured), but the vast majority of people in the country had to pay higher premiums for their health insurance.[xv]

Because of the higher cost of health insurance, many Christians shifted to an alternative to traditional health insurance called health sharing. Health Sharing Plans are not insurance in the conventional sense; there is no intermediary like Humana paying the hospitals and collecting premiums. The health-sharing model is set up so that members pay each other's claims through an organized, rules-based system. Sounds weird, right? Well, it's a legitimate system with a respectable track record. One of the largest groups, Medishare, has paid over $4 billion in bills since 1993.[xvi] In fact, despite my hesitancy, our family enrolled in this program and subsequently had a family illness that resulted in over $100,000 in medical bills. Without an issue, those bills were paid entirely through the health-sharing program.

Let me give you an example of how the various programs work. Let's say the Ford family from Florida signs up for one of the Christian health-sharing programs. Every month they send their financial commitment (similar to a premium) directly to another family across the country. Let's call this family who receives the check the Travis family in Texas. The Travis family is on the receiving end of this health-sharing relationship because their daughter fell off a horse, broke her ankle, and they subsequently have multiple medical bills. The Travis family received a stack of doctor and hospital invoices but hasn't paid them because they have been waiting for the health-sharing checks. When the Ford family's check and other families' checks arrive in the mail, the Travis family has enough to pay their medical bills in full. Of course, the system can be automated with Electronic Funds Transfer payment services and other internal portals. Still, the physical check-writing system gives you an illustration of the money flow.

Even though the system is different, and a change from a traditional health insurance model is uncomfortable, many people take the plunge to benefit from the considerable monthly premium savings by removing the insurance intermediary.

Let's look at the comparable alternatives in the marketplace.

For traditional insurance with a standard carrier like Blue Cross Blue Shield, according to healthcare.gov, a family of four with a $150,000 combined income would pay $1,088 per month in insurance premiums for a bronze plan. They may qualify for a tax credit of $492, so their net premium would be $596 per month. The insurance company wouldn't cover a dime until the $17,400 family deductible was met and, of course, if they stayed within their designated network.[xvii]

With the health-sharing alternative programs, health-share company #1 has a model for the same family profile that costs $351 per month with a $12,000 annual household obligation before the medical bills are covered.[xviii]

Health share company #2 can reduce the premium even more to $255 per month and offer a lower deductible of $5,000 before expenses are paid.[xix]

As a final example, health-share company #3 has a monthly obligation of $596 per month for that same family and will pay for a medical event once the cost for that event exceeds $400.[xx]

It's important to note that these programs have treatment limits, considerations for excluding preexisting conditions, and other nuances that require further examination. However, the above information gives you an idea of alternative health-care choices for the Christian family.

Regarding tax deductions, currently, traditional insurance is considered an itemized deduction once it exceeds 7.5% of your income for the year. The guidance on the deductibility for the health-sharing programs hasn't been explicitly clear, and proposed regulations attempt to memorialize the health-sharing tax deductibility within the same framework as traditional health insurance. Most people follow the guidance of their CPA or tax preparer.[xxi]

This alternative to the current system is gaining momentum and is on the verge of exploding because it helps ease the premium burden on America's middle-class families. According to the Health Care Cost Institute, from 2012 to 2016, the national average price level of health care grew by 16%.[xxii] That's 16% annually! While politicians focus on peripheral issues, the continued increase in health insurance premiums is the most significant burden on the middle class.

But why are Christians willing to take the risk and go outside the mainstream system? It's because they trust each other. Christians trust that those operating the organization to facilitate the exchange of money are doing it within the framework of Christian principles, not rooted in greed or selfish ambition. This element of trust is the critical ingredient of the program and is why the entire Christian community is moving toward this alternative platform.

Frankly, if our country doesn't fix our healthcare system, millions of families will be subject to years of burdensome medical debt. As we'll find out next, Christians are allergic to debt.

Continuing the Conversation

There are now non-Christian sharing programs available in the marketplace. For a long time, you had to attest to church attendance to be a member of the Christian sharing programs. Some health-sharing programs still require those qualifications, but others are more flexible and even available to the non-Christian community. I encourage every family to look at alternative solutions to traditional health insurance.

"The rich rule over the poor,
and the borrower is slave of the lender."

Proverbs 22:7

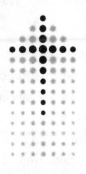

CHAPTER 6:

Allergic to Debt

I f you search "debt" on Google or YouTube, it won't take long to discover the Tennessee radio personality named Dave Ramsey. Ramsey has earned a reputation for motivating thousands, if not millions, of Americans to cut up credit cards and pay off homes. Families road trip across the country to Dave's home office in Franklin, Tennessee, to shake his hand and scream with tears in their eyes, "I'm debt-free!" Maybe it's jealousy, but some financial experts resent his rigid recommendations. With his simplified motivational money message, the truth is that this commonsense guy from Tennessee has inspired more people than any financial advisor . . . ever.

Dave Ramsey is an unapologetic Christian who would be categorized as a Practicing Christian. He has a public track record of following the faith from the giving to the living. But, because Dave is a Practicing Christian and hates debt as much as a cat hates falling into a pool of cold water, does that mean borrowing money is evil? I mean, nearly every business school preaches the art of leveraging. Is leveraging and acquiring debt strategically and even prudently a sin subject to eternal damnation? Of course not. Debt is not a sin, and Christians aren't subject to punishment if they get a mortgage, borrow money for a business startup, or even if they messed up by overspending on their AMEX.

Even though it isn't a sin, there is enough concrete advice in the ancient texts from Jewish scholars who acknowledge that debt can be very dangerous no matter how smart, clever, or successful you might think you are. Many families have been generationally damaged because someone along the family tree (usually a man) got cute with debt. The only ones who profess the joy of debt are those who've never been burned before, but many (including those Jewish scholars) with debt scars call debt dangerous.

Most of the time, debt by Christians is used in the most prudent way possible to acquire something that requires a ton of cash, like a home or a business. However, shortly after the debt is incurred and shows up on a statement, things get real for the Christian. They get that kinda sick feeling in their stomach because they remember and believe that "the borrower is a slave to the lender." That sick feeling will motivate every Christian to accelerate the debt payoff.

Many times, debt is the only way to pay medical bills. One major unpredictable event could push a family over the edge into bankruptcy. According to a recent Kaiser Family Foundation poll, about one in five Americans are paying off bills for a family member's care through an installment plan with a hospital or other provider.[xxiii] No one would fault a mom or dad who wipes out their emergency fund and maxes out MasterCard to find an alternative cancer treatment for their child.

But if Christians rack up a pile of medical debt on their credit cards, they plan to repay it. They will customize the terms, negotiate the rates, ask for discounts, and find a way to pay off the debt. Christians are given straightforward advice from a New Testament guy named Paul when he said, "Let no debt remain unpaid." [xxiv] Some people suggest that you should borrow as much as you can, and if you can't repay it, then simply reset your life by declaring bankruptcy. However, many Christians won't consider bankruptcy, defaults, or foreclosures as initial options because there is honor in repayment. But, as it is for many families, these relief solutions are sometimes the only way out. Just know that the internal struggle is real for the Christian. Christians will have sleepless nights balancing this sense of honor with the harsh reality that their family could be financially burdened by lifetime of debt.

We will need to recognize the cautious Christian perspective on debt while also understanding the situational needs for which it can be used with prudence. Over time, I have realized that the ankle chains of debt are incredibly burdensome to families. Christians will reach a point where they become highly motivated to take those chains off and experience the freedom of living debt-free.

The reality of life is that some of us will get our debts resolved because we inherited money from mom and dad. No one can fault family wealth being passed down. But you may be at fault if you mess it up by not critically and intentionally designing your wills and trusts. We'll look at legacy planning next.

Continuing the Conversation

In my early twenties, I didn't think much of Dave Ramsey because I was a "sophisticated financial guy" with a CFP™ after my name. That thought changed when I found myself up to my ears in credit card debt. To get out, my wife and I diligently and religiously implemented the practice of Dave's baby steps and cash envelopes. It was a game-changer for my family, and we were able to overcome the financial burdens of debt payments. Over the years, I've learned to appreciate his approach and would encourage every family to go through Financial Peace University.

> "A good person leaves an inheritance
> for their children's children, but a sinner's
> wealth is stored up for the righteous."
> *Proverbs 13:22*

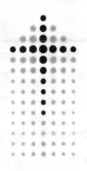

CHAPTER 7:

The Transfer of Multigenerational Wealth

B
aby boomers will transfer more than $30 trillion of wealth to the next generation through gifts and inheritances over the next two decades. [xxv] This transfer is one of the most significant wealth transitions in history. In fact, the fortunate population who will receive this money accounts for 136 million people. If you are one of those 136

million recipients, you might get a check for $220,000 when a parent passes away ($30 trillion/136 million people).[xxvi]

How will Christians uniquely approach this significant responsibility of transferring their wealth?

For affluent people, there comes a point when you must ask yourself, "How much is enough?" This question is certainly not limited to the Christian community. No one wants to die with a mattress full of money and have their ex-son-in-law blow the family's life savings on a Vegas Superbowl bet—Christian or not. Even beyond the practical considerations, the Christian community approaches an inheritance as a holy transaction. Traditionally, in the Old Testament texts, an inheritance was so sacred that it wasn't allowed to pass from one tribe to another.[xxvii] Today, Christians don't necessarily view the idea of inheritance with the same rigidity. Still, they cannot help but recognize the potential impact of an intentional generational wealth transfer.

In my experience, the Christian community views an inheritance as a legacy. An inheritance is what you leave to someone, whereas a legacy is what you leave in someone. Leaving "in someone" means that one's values are transferred, just like Moses passed down the Ten Commandments to generations afterward. So, when Christians think about an inheritance (the money part), planning out the legacy (the values part) is equally essential. For example, suppose a grandmother anchors to the Christian tenet that considers hard work a righteous and honorable attribute. If her son is lazy and unwilling to get a job, she knows that an inheritance may accentuate this sedentary behavior. She will not leave her son money that causes unemployment and laziness, no matter how much she loves him. Warren Buffett said it very well when asked how he would give money to the next generation: "Leave the children enough to do anything but not enough so they do nothing."

So, how can a Christian legally orchestrate their legacy to ensure that the money extends these sacred values? A simple will is one solution. The benefit of a will is that it is generally low-cost and easy to execute. The challenge for people with a lot of money is that this legal document doesn't have the flexibility to construct the details of personalized values requests.

Therefore, seeking legal counsel from an attorney may be necessary to see if a trust is suitable for the Christian family. Granted, living trusts cost more money to set up and require a bit more maintenance, but for someone with many assets, this is likely to be the legacy tool of choice. With a living trust, the family can customize who receives the money, how much, and under what conditions. Then, should circumstances change, the Christian can help alter the terms of the trust without retitling assets and redoing the entire legal document.

For example, suppose a family is concerned about their son's wife, who has a track record of behaviors that are misaligned with their family's values . . . she's a constant drunk, gossips, and lies . . . let's say she's not a good person. As a result, the parents could write in the living trust that if their son passes away, they do not want his inheritance to be given to the daughter-in-law but directly to the grandchildren with the help of a trustee. Suppose the daughter-in-law turns her life around, and their relationship is restored; the family could then remove the original restraining terms from the living trust, knowing their legacy/inheritance would not be undermined.

Many other legal frameworks are available, but a living trust is a tool that should be considered as a way to pass wealth to the next generation. Much of the Old Testament content emphasizes the importance of considering the generational impact when making decisions. As a result of these teachings, the Christian's motivation when leaving money as an inheritance is not just about providing for personal pleasure, but rather it's a way to memorialize values for multiple generations.

Unfortunately, con artists know about this massive legacy trend and are trying to intercept the money before the kids inherit it. Let's talk about this significant threat in further detail.

Continuing the Conversation

When you pass away, you can give your money to family, charity, or the IRS. If you plan today, you do have some choice in the matter. Everyone should invest a little time being intentional about who gets how much. Of course, disinheriting the IRS should be a priority; then the final, critical question will be, "How much money and assets go to my family and how much to ministry/charity?"

> "Watch out for false prophets.
> They come to you in sheep's clothing,
> but inwardly they are ferocious wolves."
> *Matthew 7:15*

Controlling the Conversation

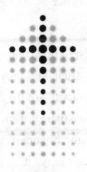

CHAPTER 8:

Financial Con Artists

The notorious bank robber Willie Sutton was asked by a reporter why he robbed banks, and his reply was, "That's where the money is." As stated in this book, the scope of wealth held by the Christian community is enormous (55% of the world's wealth), and that is where the money is. If you combine this scope of wealth with a Christian community that is quick to trust others, you have a situation ripe for con artists—the con artist who carries a Bible.

Bible-carrying con artists know that the currency within the Christian community is trust, and they exploit it.

Some of those con artists are disguised as financial advisors. Because many Christians are motivated to save (as discussed previously), many financial advisors will target the audience at church. For many, it is part of their marketing strategy. I love going to church, but it is a sacred time for me, and I prefer not to talk about money or business while worshiping. But for the financial advisor con artist, hallway talk at church is their preferred strategy. These sick financial advisors will join a men's group or a Bible study with the sole purpose of solicitation, and they are so smooth that it's hard to distinguish their insincerity.

Recently, within our community, there was a financial advisor who was highly visible and ran very professional commercials that elevated his reputation. His public profile created a perception of credibility. As a result, he convinced many Christians in the community to invest, not in publicly traded securities, but rather in his own business. He used elderly clients' retirement money to buy the commercials and perpetuate his image! When I realized the scope of his scheme, I searched his background on the FINRA website (https://brokercheck.finra.org/). I noticed a material misrepresentation in his public background stated on the FINRA website compared to his "about me" page on his public-facing website. The regulators didn't take long to crack down, fine him, and serve him jail time. However, many Christian clients never recovered their lifetime of savings.

Second, because Christians are motivated by stewardship, they are ripe for con artists to mislead them into buying into a startup. We had another situation in our community where a con artist with a Bible was moving money from clients' retirement accounts into startup companies. Very educated and sophisticated investors were allured into owning part of the next Apple, Bank of America, or Facebook. They always regretted the time decades ago when they had passed on the opportunity to buy companies in their startup phase, and these investors didn't want to miss out twice. However, they didn't know this businessperson was getting a very handsome commission for soliciting worthless company stock. The companies were ridden with high debt, low revenue, and negative cash flow. The Securities and Exchange Commission (SEC) eventually spoiled his scheme, but good Christian people lost millions of their retirement savings.

As the movement of Christians being intentional with their money grows, more and more con artists will come preying—not praying—and take advantage of trust. We all need to be on the lookout for con artists in the Christian community. They could be self-proclaimed Christian financial advisors who have obtained the proper licensing but operate with unauthentic motives. Or they could be friends from church soliciting capital for a new venture beyond the scope of a client's risk tolerance. We must all work together to protect our friends, the elderly, and the community from these con artists carrying a Bible.

Continuing the Conversation

I admit that even though I'm a pretty nice guy, I get angry now and then. My anger manifests into ugly outrage when I see a Christian brother or sister go to a Bible study and then get misled into an unnecessary, unsuitable, or fraudulent financial investment. Over the years, I've met too many fraudsters, and they continue to prey on my peers. If I find one, I'll make sure these guys lose their licenses or get jailed.

> "Whatever you do, work at it with all your heart, as working for the Lord, not for human masters."
> *Colossians 3:23*

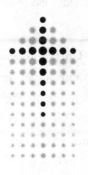

CHAPTER 9:

Don't Retire–Pivot

We are seeing a trend develop since 2020 of retirees slowly returning to work.[xxviii] Are Christian retirees returning to work, or did they never retire in the first place? It's difficult to dissect this marketplace, but what we can do is dig into the Christian's motivation not to retire, to retire, or to unretire and better understand the biblical context that drives retirement decisions.

The challenge for Christians is that their ancient texts only mention retirement once. In all sixty-six books, there is only one reference to the idea of "retire." You can find it in the Torah (the first five books of the Bible). In this text, Moses (not to be confused with Noah, who built the ark) and the Levites were to stop doing physical labor and let the younger people start bending their backs instead.[xxix]

So, like Moses, many of us must retire because our body, mind, and sometimes our back tell us that it's time. To prepare for this future date, Christian and non-Christian Americans are motivated to save enough money so we can stop working and live off our savings.

I say all this because the Christian worldview, like most Americans, acknowledges a certain point in life when our health requires us to transition from a prior career.

I would contend that the Christian, because of their faith, is exceptionally well-equipped for retirement since their identity is not rooted in their occupation but in their unique life purpose bestowed upon them by their Creator. This sense of purpose seems immaterial to many, but it is a fundamental tenet of faith. Christians believe every person has a unique purpose and that if there is breath in your lungs, your Creator still has a plan for your life.

The Christian reflects and says to himself, "I know exactly why I'm getting up in the morning. It's because my Creator has a purpose for me, and I need to lean into that purpose and get the job done." The Christian retiree will pivot into the next chapter of life, knowing that their life experiences have equipped them with wisdom, hopefully, a little money, and now time. Combining these three things puts them in a unique position to love their neighbor like never before.

Many of my retired friends have discontinued using the word "retirement" because it implies the end of a useful life and have replaced that word with "pivot." Pivoting into the next chapter of life infers new opportunities and enthusiasm. In 2021, I wanted to capture some of these pivot stories by interviewing recent retirees through my podcast, Retire In Texas. Here are just a few of those stories:

Valinda didn't retire from business; she pivoted into rescuing trafficked children.

Neal didn't retire from management; he pivoted into becoming a city councilman.

Barbara didn't retire from the service industry; she pivoted into being a baby cuddler at a local hospital.

Mark didn't retire from his career as a CPA; he pivoted into becoming a consultant.

I literally have hundreds of stories of people who refuse to retire because they believe God still has a purpose for their lives. How they find this purpose is a personal discovery process, but there isn't a doubt that these Christians are on a new mission. They are ready for what God will do in and through them. So, as we see these baby boomers transition out of retirement, prepare for a massive movement of Christian silver hairs ready and willing to live out their purpose.

To properly navigate these challenging retirement decisions, we need the help of financial institutions. Let's discover how they innovate and create new tools to help us think through the various chapters of life.

Continuing the Conversation

The other day, a client said, "When I retire in a few years, I want to work at Walmart because I've always wanted to greet people when they walk in." I know this person's finances, and I know they have enough money to never work again. I found it refreshing for someone to say aloud, "I don't care what others say, this is my dream, and I'm going to do it." Being active, engaging with others, and living out a retirement vision is much more exciting than Fox News and flowerbeds.

> "Let your conversation be always full of grace,
> seasoned with salt, so that you may know
> how to answer everyone."
> *Colossians 4:6*

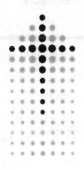

CHAPTER 10

Behavioral Finance

I n the 1980s, financial institutions hired smart stockbrokers and sold you stocks because you didn't have the information and tools to buy them. Then, the internet gave you the knowledge and the tools to trade stocks.

Power to the people.

So, then financial institutions created asset allocation models, which added value to your life because they could build a portfolio with all the different investments for all types of people. Then, people used computer algorithms to make the asset allocations work even better.

Power back to the people.

Today, after losing the gatekeeper of information status, institutions have finally found how to deliver authentic value —personal financial advice. This advice is delivered in such a way that it safeguards against irrational human money behaviors like selling stocks at the bottom of a market. Vanguard calls this Advisor Alpha, and their research suggests it can provide an additional 3% net returns to clients.[xxx]

But we must ask, if the banks and money firms move into a personal finance model, can a non-Christian financial person at a bank help guide Christians with their unique money motivations? The answer is a resounding yes. Can a neurosurgeon work on a brain without performing brain surgery? Can a bankruptcy attorney help a broke business owner if the attorney has never filed Chapter 7 or Chapter 11? Can a straight financial advisor help a gay couple? Can a conservative help a liberal? Yes! We can work together in the financial space with differing opinions while respecting the other's point of view.

You don't need to be a Bible scholar to advise Christians; you just need to understand, honor, and respect their sacred motivations. For a financial institution to serve a Christian family, the solution to discover a Christian's money motives can be found by adopting a personal finance model that facilitates dialogue and avoids confrontation.

Historically, financial professionals would use factfinders as the preferred discovery method for uncovering beliefs, desires, and money motives. Unfortunately, these traditional finance tools fell short because they would make assumptions or, at the very least, fail to memorialize a family's values and priorities. Most of the time, they were just boring. They gathered information about life insurance, cash, and investments and gave birth to an equally boring set of financial recommendations. However, in recent years, through the outstanding work of Kahneman and Tversky, behavioral economics has elevated the personal finance experience for everyone. This area of academic study acknowledges the physical makeup of the brain under stress through neuroscience. Then, it overlays this education with recognizing the deep-rooted rationale behind people's quirky money behaviors. Finally, it is based on traditional and classical personal finance areas rooted in math, compound growth, and modern portfolio theory.

Behavioral finance tools create open-ended dialogue for a financial professional to discover how to design a unique family money strategy that acknowledges and emphasizes the family's motivations, regardless of religion. For example, I have used a behavioral finance tool that identified a mother's number one priority: leaving a legacy. Her husband never once in their twenty years of marriage knew how vital that personal life mission was to her. This "financial conversation" flowed with tears absorbed by tissues. Now, with a renewed family focus, all money decisions can consider that this mother's motivation is to leave a legacy. Only a specifically designed behavioral finance tool can discover and highlight that type of heartfelt money motivation.

Each behavioral finance tool has its own unique discovery questions that tap into what God put in someone's heart. Because many of these tools were developed academically and secularly, they can allow even a non-Christian to be objective rather than tripping over an opinion and risking the relationship. Through a behavioral finance system, the professional aims to discover the family's money motivations and then identify financial strategies that align with those convictions. For example, suppose someone has a conviction that they hate (with a capital H) the IRS. In that case, the professional's job is to discover this conviction, have a conversation without a debate, and find tools such as municipal bonds or tax-deferred annuities to reduce or defer taxable income.

After years of integrating traditional fact-finding tools, our team became exhausted with boredom and limitations, so we enthusiastically adopted a behavioral finance tool from United

Capital called FINLIFE. In this framework, the conversation touches on the softer side of money rather than just returns. This approach can be unsettling to certain performance-oriented personality types, but it has allowed us to understand the "why" behind financial decisions. We have often found that the reason people have made certain decisions was a direct result of their childhood experiences. A family's motive for staying in their home for twenty-five years could be because one spouse grew up in a military family and wanted stability for their children. Another spouse might say they can't keep enough cash because, as a teen, they experienced the pain of their dad filing bankruptcy. We learn the "why" because the behavioral finance experience helps us tap into what God put on someone's heart.

Also, as an incredible bonus, behavioral exercises often have allowed us to facilitate a conversation with the meek, quiet, non-financial-minded spouse (usually the wife) whose voice was drowned out by the more assertive husband. The previous bland fact-finding tools intimated and bored the wife, who wasn't of a financial mind, but we found that her money motivation was the one that mattered the most. The non-financial-minded spouse was a voice of reason that balanced out the assertive spouse focused on maximizing returns and taking on investment bets. Although money results matter, the behavioral finance tool has allowed us to hear both perspectives so that the motivations of the entire family come to the surface.

Behavioral finance is quickly becoming the engine behind every single financial institution, but how it is delivered to the consumer varies from place to place. The beauty of the multiple techniques is that they allow people from different backgrounds to ask probing questions within the boundaries of a system that begins with a financial plan. Outside of a system and a dream, a financial professional could accidentally interject their motivations, disrupting the client experience and ultimately losing trust. In the future, behavioral finance tools will be the ultimate way all financial institutions will serve the massive movement of Christians who see money as more than math.

Through another powerful technology innovation, Christians' voice will be heard. Let's explore this tool next.

Continuing the Conversation

One of the greatest outcomes of behavioral finance is that it gives the non-CFO spouse a voice. Some spouses have a distaste for all things math and money, but their voice, passions, dreams, and goals are valuable. Many spouses' goals have a dollar sign on them and need to be accounted for in the planning, rather than discounted. Hearing from the non-CFO spouse is made possible through thoughtful questioning often built around behavioral finance. If done right, then the non-CFO spouse's voice will be heard and honored.

"I have fought the good fight,
I have finished the race, I have kept the faith."
2 Timothy 4:7

CHAPTER 11:

Proxy Voting

What happens when the motivation of a publicly traded corporation is in direct conflict with the motivation of a Christian shareholder? What if a corporation goes beyond a simple value conflict but even adopts a company policy that directly and openly restricts religious freedom? Are there any solutions to resolve this issue if you are not an internal executive or board member but, instead, are simply a shareholder that owns stock through an IRA or mutual fund? Yes, there is a solution that is being adopted more often, called a proxy vote.

One of the most underutilized rights for shareholders is the right to vote on matters affecting the company's leadership and corporate decision-making. This right is awarded to those who own individual company stock shares regardless of ownership amount. Even though this ownership is often a fractional amount relative to the millions of shareholders in a large-capitalization corporation such as Apple and Google, equity participation still allows the shareholder a voice. Most of the votes for corporations take place on-site at an annual meeting, but the idea of a proxy vote enables a shareholder to cast a vote without attending the annual meeting. The rules for providing the information necessary for shareholders to understand board recommendations are outlined in SEC Section 14 A.[xxxi]

Shareholders receive annual letters outlining board recommendations for salient corporate governance issues. These issues could be voting for a board member, a merger, or other material events. A few shareholders have elected to receive these formal letters electronically. Because snail mail has nearly become irrelevant unless you are a credit card solicitor, these letters are often misunderstood and discarded. In my two decades of experience working with clients, I rarely have clients ask about the merits of proxy voting letters. We are all busy, and if there isn't a material action affecting the price of our security, we discard the information and grab a quick meal before running our kids to a soccer game.

But what if there is a way that shareholders with a standard set of values can delegate proxy voting to a third party who understands the proxy voting process and can represent the shareholders? What if this representative can vote on behalf of tens, hundreds, or thousands of shareholders so that the voice of this collective group is slightly louder than one or two outlier dissidents? If this representative did vote with this collective voice, would it give corporations a slight pause before adopting decisions that conflict with Christian motives?

In the future, I imagine corporations will hear the Christian voice loudly through proxy votes and advocates. This advocacy for the Christian community will be essential in influencing corporate governance because, right now, the few yet louder people are completely drowning out a Christian voice, and there is no tolerance for different opinions. For example, according to a recent survey conducted by Alliance Defending Freedom, "40% of the companies surveyed discriminate against religious employees by stopping them from supporting faith-based causes in their matching-gift contributions." [xxxii]

The proxy vote must be the tool of choice for the Christian voice to be heard because it will not happen at the executive or board level. Imagine the challenge and corporate consequence of a vice president disagreeing with a company decision based on a Christian worldview. If that vice president has a minority opinion on a controversial topic, it would be an excruciating death to confront the rest of his peers who live within the same communities and hold firm, unified political opinions. However, if that executive can separate his opinion and objectively state, "Well, we have a collective proxy vote of a group of shareholders that claims this decision is antagonistic toward the Christian community. Let's hear their case." Then, the collective proxy voting group can begin a conversation with a tolerance of opinion and possibly slow any inconsideration of Christians.

What's great is that today we have the technology to allow all religious groups to elect their financial representative as proxy representatives. Companies such as Broadridge Financial Solutions have seamlessly integrated voting materials and information so that professionals or fund companies can implement this service as a part of their value offerings. This technology allows others who understand corporate governance to efficiently represent a group of Christians. I find that leaning on the fund companies to do the voting is much easier than keeping up with the individual companies. Regardless of how it's done, Christians need an advocate who understands the Christian's motives, respects religious freedom, and can highlight any board conduct considered harassment or humiliation toward people of faith.

On a go-forward basis, through proxy voting, Christians can invest according to their values and, at the same time, play a role in how companies treat Christians in the marketplace.

Continuing the Conversation

Individual proxy voting is done at the individual stock level. So, if you own individual stocks, then you have a vote. However, for mutual funds and exchange-traded funds, the fund manufacturer votes on your behalf. Please ensure the fund company shares your values. Otherwise, these big investment firms and fund companies will use your vote on what you distaste.

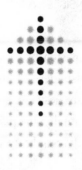

Conclusion

I heard a rumor that Layne Staley (the lead singer of Alice in Chains) died in his Los Angeles condominium with a picture of Jesus hanging tilted in Layne's isolated room. Before he died, friends soberly mentioned that Layne every bit like a heroin addict with skin on bone and a skid row of needle marks down his arms. He even made one last attempt to record a cover song, and his production team had to implement some creative editing to drown out the lisp and wisp that came from missing teeth. As I listened to his discography collection, his lyrics consistently wrestled with the conflicting worldviews and dark misunderstandings of Jesus Christ, God, and religion. I'm not sure how close he ever came to turning his life around, but eventually, the pain of living with depression and addiction finally caught up to him at the young age of thirty-four.

Most Christians are no different inside than Layne, as there is a constant battle of conflicting thoughts, worldviews, and motivations. Christians struggle daily with the temptation of personal pleasure at the expense of doing the right thing. Even though doing the right thing has been passed down from ancient authors through principles, parables, and sayings, it's still hard . . . we want stuff, and we want to feel good. Money is the most material and consequential issue where Christians are tempted to do something rooted in selfishness over loving a neighbor or honoring God. You've seen it, and I've seen it. I can't reinforce it enough . . . Christians are like everyone else. We all have a natural, internal motivation conflict, and we must battle every day against the desire to consume, hoard, and consume again at the expense of the calling to be a good steward.

But having a standard of right and wrong that may seem narrow to many brings freedom to the Christian. Practicing Christians quickly get pricked by a conscience that says, "You may mess up today, but long term, keep doing your best to put Jesus's motives ahead of your own." Through community, content, and the art of being still, Christians steadfastly pursue the idea of loving their neighbor and honoring God.

This faith that resolves internal conflicts has existed for thousands of years, and it is quite a miracle that the people of the Way continue to hold tight to the idea of stewardship above pleasure. For generations, the people of the Way have had a different motivation for saving, a sacred approach to legacy, and a skeptical view of debt. Working with Christians over the years, I have learned much about the Christian worldview of money by example. I have witnessed the peace when someone loses money from fraud or bad business decisions, the kindness in giving without recognition, and even the hope when losing a child. I have seen business owners restrict their income to provide for others and sacrifice personal lifestyles so employees can have a better life. I've seen material and substantial gifts made private when they could have been celebrated. I've sat down with seniors who live only on social security, commit to giving monthly, and live happier lives than people with millions who hoard. I've seen situations where a Christian should have sued for recourse but passed on the attorney's request because peace was more important than money. I've seen the poor receive private checks from

Christians and groceries paid for without knowing who the benefactor was.

If America's money motivations are consumption, pleasure, and hoarding, then I suggest that the Christian's money motivations should be more than just respected and honored—they should be modeled. If the fruit of American consumerism simply yields a legacy of anxiety, maybe there is something to learn and adopt from the money motives of the people of the Way.

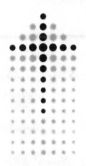

Q&A WITH THE AUTHOR:

A Peek behind the Curtain

Michelle Booth: When did you begin integrating faith into your financial advisory services?

Darryl Lyons: I didn't want to integrate them initially because I always thought about the businesspeople who put a fish on their card and then took advantage of people's trust. I despised the person who used faith to get the business. It took over twenty years for me to get over those hesitations. But I finally did it, and I have never felt more excited and more sincere about our role in peoples' lives.

Michelle Booth: Why was it important to you to make the change?

Darryl Lyons: I became really frustrated seeing unethical financial people take advantage of my Christian friends. Large financial institutions neglecting or even undermining Christian values made me equally frustrated. So, I desire to fill a gap in the marketplace where our country finally has a trustworthy financial institution that honors and respects Judeo-Christian values.

Michelle Booth: How has it impacted your business?

Darryl Lyons: I'm blown away by the growth and appetite for our services. We went from a small company in San Antonio, Texas, to having clients nationwide. The key to our continued growth and success is attracting many more intelligent financial professionals who respect the faith and are excited about the mission.

Michelle Booth: Do you find yourself offending others who disagree with you?

Darryl Lyons: Not really; most people respect our values. I think when I was wishy-washy about my positioning, that's when I offended people. People appreciate sincerity, and I've learned that to be unclear is to be unkind. Kindness is one of our core values; a little kindness goes a long way.

Michelle Booth: You speak a lot about being a fiduciary. Is there a conflict when integrating your faith into your investment recommendations?

Darryl Lyons: It can be a conflict, so you must be careful. We don't adopt investment or financial advice solutions that violate our fiduciary responsibility. If Biblically Responsible Investing is unreasonably expensive and performs poorly, we aren't adding that solution, no matter how much the company loves Jesus. We have a job to do, and when we do that job well, God is honored.

Michelle Booth: Does that mean that all employees of PAX are Christians?

Darryl Lyons: I honestly don't know. We have government rules to follow, so it's not a hiring question or part of performance reviews. I can tell you that everyone at PAX truly honors and respects Christian values. Ultimately, I hope everyone on the team will become Christian along with their children and their children's children. But, as a CEO, I must play by the rules, so I let my leadership and heart do much of the talking.

Michelle Booth: What are your company growth plans?

Darryl Lyons: Our ambition is to serve ten thousand families. We have plenty of capacity as long as we attract the right talented employees and competent financial advisors who want to be a part of our mission. I expect that PAX will become a household name soon.

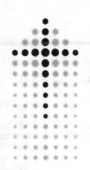

About the Author

arryl Lyons is considered an expert in personal finance and small business. He has authored several books, including *Small Business Big Pressure*, *The Grand Money Chasm*, and *18 to 80: A Simple and Practical Guide to Money and Retirement for All Ages*. Darryl is also a contributing writer for Forbes and other local publications. He is the host of the popular podcast, Retire in Texas.

As CEO and co-founder, Darryl has led PAX Financial Group to consistent growth recognized multiple times through Inc. 5000 "Fastest Growing Companies." Among PAX's many accolades, Darryl is most proud of the San Antonio Business Journal naming PAX Financial Group as one of the "Best Places to Work" in the city.

Darryl received the San Antonio North Chamber's Small Businessperson of the Year award for his focus on mentoring others, including those who served our country and are frontline officers. A community leader, Mayor Julian Castro, recognized Darryl for his involvement in redeveloping a part of the city by naming Darryl W. Lyons Park in his honor. He also helped start a non-profit in Eastern Europe that helps kids get off the streets and onto the basketball court. The ministry is called "The Admirals," named after NBA Hall of Famer David Robinson. Darryl is a Certified Financial Planner™ (CFP), an Accredited Investment Fiduciary ™ (AIF), a Behavioral Financial Advisor (BFA), and a Chartered Financial Consultant (ChFC). He completed his bachelor's in business administration in Accounting and Corporate Finance at St. Mary's University and received his master's in jurisprudence (MJ) through Texas A&M Law School.

Darryl enjoys listening to his 90s music, nerding out on his sports collection, and reading. His family of six live in New Braunfels, TX, and they enjoy hunting, fishing, being outdoors in small towns, pet slobber, and all things Texas Hill Country.

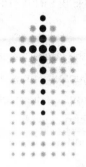

References

i   "Race, Religion Key Indicators of US Political Affil-
    iation," Good Faith Media, June 24, 2020, https://
    goodfaithmedia.org/race-religion-key-indicators-
    of-us-political-affiliation/.

ii From the website of the U.S.Equal Employment
    Opportunity Commission, "Section 12: Religious Dis-
    crimination," January 15, 2021, https://www.eeoc.gov/
    laws/guidance/section-12-religious-discrimination.

iii   "Christians hold the largest percentage of global wealth: Report," The Economic Times, January 14, 2105, https://economictimes.indiatimes.com/news/company/corporate-trends/christians-hold-largest-percentage-of-global-wealth-report/articleshow/45886471.cms.

iv   "CRC Report Finds Nearly 70% of AmericansClaim to be 'Christian,' But What Does That Mean?," by Tracy Munsil, Arizona Christian University, August 31, 2021, https://www.arizonachristian.edu/2021/08/31/crc-report-finds-nearly-70-of-americans-claim-to-be-christian-but-what-does-that-mean/#:~:text=Barna%20explained%20that%20the%20broader,and%20voting%20behavior%20of%20Christians.

v   The American Bible Society blog, "Our New Study Shows Important Distinctions Between Self-Identified and Practicing Christians," October 14, 2021, https://news.americanbible.org/blog/entry/corporate-blog/new-study-shows-important-distinctions-between-christians.

vi   "Disney lowers longer-term forecast for Disney+ subscribers by 15 million," by Alex Sherman, CNBC, last updated August 10, 2022, https://www.cnbc.com/2022/08/10/disney-lowers-2024-forecast-for-disney-subscribers-by-15-million.html

vii   "Does Socially Responsible Investing Hurt Investment Returns?," RBC Global Asset Management, https://funds.rbcgam.com/_assets-custom/pdf/RBC-GAM-does-SRI-hurt-investment-returns.pdf.

viii   "CIF Fund Permance Study 2020," Faith Driven Investor, https://www.faithdriveninvestor.org/content-page/cif-fund-performance-study-2020.

ix   "State of the Bible USA 2022," from the American Bible Society, https://1s712.americanbible.org/state-of-the-bible/stateofthebible/State_of_the_bible-2022.pdf.

x   From the website of the IRS, "IRA FAQs – Distributions (Withdrawals)." https://www.irs.gov/retirement-plans/retirement-plans-faqs-regarding-iras-distributions-withdrawals

xi   From the website of the IRS, "Actuarial Tables." https://www.irs.gov/retirement-plans/actuarial-tables

xii   From the website of the IRS, "Topic No. 551 Standard Deduction." https://www.irs.gov/taxtopics/tc551

xiii   "Report + FAQs," Unmasking Fidelity, https://unmaskingfidelity.org/report-faqs/

xiv   Project Publications // Science of Generosity // University of Notre Dame (nd.edu), accessed 3/30/2023 1:40 pm CST

xv "The Medi-Share Difference," Medi-Share, https://www.medishare.org/medishare-difference/.

xvi "The Medi-Share Difference," Medi-Share, https://www.medishare.org/medishare-difference/.

xvii "See Plans & Prices," HealthCare.gov, https://www.healthcare.gov/see-plans/#/.

xviii "The Medi-Share Difference," Medi-Share, https://www.medishare.org/medishare-difference/.

xix "CHM costs and programs," Christian Healthcare Ministries, https://chministries.org/programs-costs/.

xx "Samaritan™ Classic/Basic Cost Calculator," Samaritan Ministries, https://samaritanministries.org/classicbasic/cost.

xxi "Certain Medical Care Arrangements," FederalRegister.gov, https://www.federalregister.gov/documents/2020/06/10/2020-12213/certain-medical-care-arrangements

xxii "Understanding how price growth affected areas differently across the country," by Kevin Kennedy and William Johnson, Health Care Cost Institute, October 24, 2018, https://healthcostinstitute.org/hcci-research/hmi-2018-prive-level-v-growth?highlight=WyJwcmljZSIsImluZmxhdGlvbiJd.

xxiii "100 Million People in America Are Saddled With Health Care Debt," by Noam N. Levey, Kaiser Health News, https://khn-org.cdn.ampproject.org/c/s/khn.org/news/article/diagnosis-debt-investigation-100-million-americans-hidden-medical-debt/amp/.

xxiv The Bible Gateway website. https://www.biblegateway.com/passage/?search=Romans%2013%3A8&version=NIV

xxv "The Greatest Wealth Transfer In History: What's Happening And What Are The Implications," by Mark Hall, Forbes, November 11, 2019, https://www.forbes.com/sites/markhall/2019/11/11/the-greatest-wealth-transfer-in-history-whats-happening-and-what-are-the-implications/?sh=4e6552d84090.

xxvi "Taking advantage of the coming Great Wealth Transfer," by Wes Moss, The Atlanta Journal Constitution, April

xxvii BibleHub.com. https://biblehub.com/numbers/36-9.htm

xxviii "'Unretirements' Continue to Rise as More Workers Return to Work," by Nick Bunker, Hiring Lab, April 14, 2022, https://www.hiringlab.org/2022/04/14/unretirements-rise/.

xxix BibleHub.com. https://biblehub.com/numbers/8-24.htm

xxx From the Vanguard website. https://advisors.vanguard.com/advisors-alpha/

xxxi From the website of the U.S. Securities and Exchange Commission, "Universal Proxy, A Small Entity Compliance Guide," https://www.sec.gov/corpfin/universal-proxy-secg.

xxxii From the website of Viewpoint Diversity Score. https://viewpointdiversityscore.org/

A free ebook edition is available with the purchase of this book.

To claim your free ebook edition:

1. Visit MorganJamesBOGO.com
2. Sign your name CLEARLY in the space
3. Complete the form and submit a photo of the entire copyright page
4. You or your friend can download the ebook to your preferred device

Print & Digital Together Forever.

Snap a photo

Free ebook

Read anywhere